LOVE SPELLS

AN ENCHANTING SPELL BOOK OF POTIONS & RITUALS

Minerva Radcliffe

WELLFLEET
PRESS

Introduction

Love is the most powerful magic that exists. It connects us to other people, other beings, and to the forces of the Universe. We, as people, were made to love, and because love is an integral part of who we are, we can funnel it into our craft to attract it, receive it, and send it out. Spells are synonymous with praying and visualizing. A spell speaks an affirmation to the Universe, through our intentions, of what we want to accomplish, and how we want our lives to change.

Love spells differ from other types of witchcraft in the sense that they focus primarily on other people, rather than ourselves. Because of this, it's imperative to use them carefully. Love spells are never meant to, and should not be used to, control others or force your desires onto anyone. Doing this can harm not only the other person but you as well. You don't know what Spirit has in store for them, or you, so interfering with someone's life and free will may divert them from their otherwise perfect path.

You might inadvertently delay meeting the love of your life because you're stubbornly chasing after someone else! Here, we will show you how to use spells carefully, focus on yourself, and gently add some loving magic to your life and your relationships.

This book opens with romantic love. This is the stuff of dreams; the kind of love that makes you sigh and crack a goofy smile. It's probably what you think of when you want to fall in love. Chapter one provides spells that will help you attract, find, and enhance romantic love in your life. If you're searching for a new love but have yet to find it, this chapter will have the spells you need to give you and your future partner big heart eyes.

Moving into Chapter two, we discuss maintaining and fostering long-term love. This is the mature love that has moved past all the initial magic and has grown into something that has roots.

Unlike infatuation, long-term love stems from a deeper understanding of the other person. With that comes challenges— loss of intimacy, difficulty tackling conflict, and falling into a routine. The spells within these pages will guide you to physically care for a loved one, sample herbal magic, and advise on specific crystals to carry with you to promote long-lasting love.

The third part of this book tackles relationship troubles. It's not the easiest part of love, but every relationship has them. Conflicts aren't inherent signs of things going wrong, but instead are normal parts of every partnership. There are times when all that's needed is a simple sit-down to address unresolved issues. Other times, forgiveness is necessary. And then there are the times when all that's left is a broken heart. Chapter three will counsel you through the more unpleasant parts of love so that you can remain healthy and open.

In the last chapter we touch on the platonic love in our lives—our families, friends, and the beasts of the Earth. Platonic love occurs everywhere, and it is what we're surrounded by for most of our lives. This love is no less work than romantic love, and because it's a foundational love, it deserves just as much attention. So, in Chapter four you'll discover how to express your love through letters, how to celebrate in Nature, and to be grateful for the wondrous people and animals who surround you.

In this book, whatever you are looking for, you will find, as long as you keep your heart and mind open and do no harm. Remember, the stronger your emotions and desires are, the stronger the spell. May you find all the love that you need.

SO MOTE IT BE.*

1

Finding Romance

FINDING AND KEEPING ROMANCE IN your life can be a struggle. In this chapter, you'll explore the spells you need to discover a partner, to keep your relationship a happy one, and to bring newfound excitement and passion into a partnership.

Sure, there are common ways of finding romance, but as witches we find it by petitioning the Universe. Here, you will call not only on the love goddesses Freya and Venus, but you will also solicit the Moon herself with offerings and invitations to be present with you. Invoking these goddesses and Mother Moon leaves you with a variety of ways to attract that special someone. Because their specialty is love, they'll know how to help you best.

If you're a kitchen witch, you'll find a variety of herbs and recipes to add the finishing touches on a meal, advice on which herb to carry around with you, or how to make anointing oils for yourself and your tools—all to bring love closer to you. Herbs like basil, rosemary, dill, and lavender are all conducive to love, whether it's calming, passionate, protective, caring, or giving way to marriage. Herbal spells can provide the kind of love needed for romance.

New Moon, New Romance

If your bedroom is seeing a little too much sleep and not quite enough romance, take a moment to search your heart for what's really important in a romantic partner. Gather a small bouquet: fern for magic; ivy for fidelity; red rose for passion. Set your intentions accordingly. Invite the New Moon to sit and reflect on the chance for new beginnings. If the Moon sees into your true and good heart, her guidance is given freely.

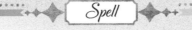

Spell

New love I seek to fill my heart, my home, my life.
A love that sparks, and grows, and lasts through good times and the strife.
A love that honors you and me, a love that with passion burns,
I seek, dear Moon, your growing light, my lover's face upturned.

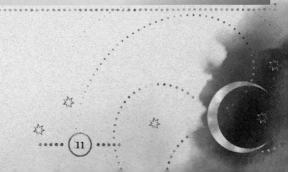

Dill Love Spell

Attracting new love can be as simple as heading into the kitchen and whipping up a little love charm. If you have dill as part of your spice cabinet arsenal, then you should know that it's a great herb to make sure love is in the air. It is also a vigorous grower and prolific self-seeder, indicating powers of fertility. Attract love and romance (and a little lust) with dill's fresh scent, which can also bring you back into emotional and mental balance when times are not so heady.

Add a few sprigs to love potions, cocktails, or food to turn on the love charm. Line windowsills to keep out negative energy. Sprinkle on food to charm your guests, or on your altar for good luck. Add seeds to charm bags for love spells. This airy plant just makes you feel good . . . sow some seeds where you can as you sow your intentions along with them and watch what happens.

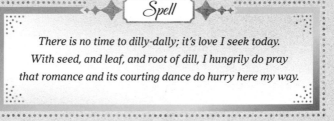

Spell

There is no time to dilly-dally; it's love I seek today.
With seed, and leaf, and root of dill, I hungrily do pray
that romance and its courting dance do hurry here my way.

True Love Spell

If things feel a little lackluster in the romance department and it's what's missing from a fully magical life, open your heart and mind to the many possibilities around you. Turn to your crystals for a little energy nudge to get things flowing. Consider stashing them by your bedside, under your pillow, or on an altar set up in your bedroom dedicated to love and romance.

Choose from:

♦ Amethyst, to soothe conflict, if that's what's in your way.
♦ Blue lace agate, which speaks from the heart; for honest communication and building trust to establish a new, or rebuild anew, relationship.

- Garnet, to stimulate passion, communicate your desires to your intended, and inspire sweep-me-off-my-feet romance.
- Malachite, which helps heal past hurts and opens your heart and mind to accept love again.
- Rose quartz, to remind you to love yourself first; others will love you in return.

Remember to clear your crystals before working with them, set your intentions, and offer thanks for their help.

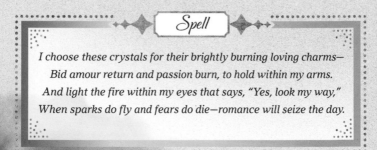

Spell

I choose these crystals for their brightly burning loving charms—
Bid amour return and passion burn, to hold within my arms.
And light the fire within my eyes that says, "Yes, look my way,"
When sparks do fly and fears do die—romance will seize the day.

Love on the Go

Because you never know when or where you might meet that one true love, pack a spell charm to take on the go—wherever and whenever—to attract love your way.

Using dried herbs and essential oils, if you wish, make a love potpourri. Select from your favorite dried herbs to attract love to you, such as rosemary, lavender, saffron threads, as well as vanilla bean, and more. Combine many different herbs, or just one or two, in a love blend. Fill a red sachet bag, tie it tightly, and carry it in your purse or pocket to send love vibrations to all those around you. The person who senses the message may just be the one you've been searching for. For an extra boost, try saying this spell as you're filling the sachet:

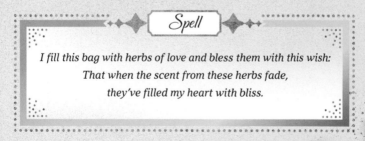

Spell

I fill this bag with herbs of love and bless them with this wish:
That when the scent from these herbs fade,
they've filled my heart with bliss.

Wishes and Dreams Jar

Whether wishing for that new person in your life or dreaming of your future with the one you already have, a wishes and dreams jar can capture the magic and preserve it to multiply. Alter the herbs, flowers, and crystals based on the energy or wish that you seek to attract to you.

Select a Mason jar with a lid, as large or as small as you like. Then, if your wish is to be married, for example, gather fresh herbs and flowers:

- ◆ Basil for luck and love
- ◆ Bee balm for compassion
- ◆ Dill for good cheer
- ◆ Ivy for marriage
- ◆ Lavender for undying devotion
- ◆ Oregano for joy
- ◆ Rosemary for remembrance
- ◆ Sage for wisdom
- ◆ Yarrow for courage and everlasting love

Add:

- ◆ Garnet for passion
- ◆ Rose petals for romance
- ◆ Your wishes written on a bay leaf

If the timing is right, place your items in a basket and infuse them overnight with the power of the New Moon to set your intentions.

Place the items in your jar, seal it, and place it on your altar, or other place you can see it, to be reminded of your wishes and dreams. When passing by, take a moment to reflect on your desires and say quietly or aloud:

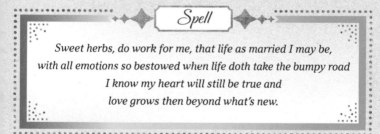

Spell

Sweet herbs, do work for me, that life as married I may be,
with all emotions so bestowed when life doth take the bumpy road
I know my heart will still be true and
love grows then beyond what's new.

To refresh your spell, light a red candle, gaze into the flame, and imagine your married life as you dream it.

Freya Love Spell

That passionate, adoring love that leaves you feeling you can tackle anything, is a magic all its own. When your desire is to ignite the flame and turn up the heat in your life, numerous love goddesses will be there to cheer you on—and Freya will be chief among them.

Spell

With runes dispersed and fates held tight,
I turn to Freya's magic sight.
Reveal when love will come my way,
when passion burns without delay.
Among the secrets of your charms,
your beauty is like a siren's call.
Teach me the tempting chant to haunt
the dreams of lovers I do want.

Catnip Love Spell

Catnip symbolizes happiness, love, and fertility; it can help attract and intoxicate a mate, as its language is love and its target is your intended.

Sprinkle the leaves over your altar when your spells target love and luck. Carry a leaf in your pocket and luck will be tempted to follow you anywhere you go. Dry larger leaves and use them as bookmarks in your spell journal. Include in sachets to amuse your cat or infuse the leaves into a tea to drink as part of a beauty ritual.

Infuse a cup of catnip tea with rose petals, sit quietly (near a camellia tree is recommended), and envision your love in as much detail as you can. When ready, say quietly or aloud:

Spell

So drunk in love I wish to be,
I sip this catnip and rose tea
whilst sitting near camellia tree
adorned with blossoms pleading thee
do nip my earlobe playfully and tell me, undeniably,
how unable you are to resist me.

Finding a Match

There is no shortage of goddess allies to offer advice on attracting the perfect mate. If that's what's on your mind, pour some wine (or tea, or other favorite beverage—one for you; one for your goddess) and settle in for a chat. You can meditate on who might be the one, journal with your goddess on taking the first step, sit outside and listen to the sounds of the Universe for cues that say the timing is right . . . whatever appeals to you. When ready, say quietly or aloud:

Spell

Bewitch me with your graceful charms and
cast a spell that does no harm.
For love is what my heart desires
and has in sight a fond admirer.
Do help me make my message clear:
I wish to bring our lips so near
that searing heat does melt our fears and
happily we'll live for years.

How Charming!

When you just can't find the right words to convey how you feel, this simple spell can help you turn on the charm. Take a moment to visualize the target of your enchantment. Take a deep calming breath and, when ready, say quietly or aloud:

Spell

Beguiling Moon, bewitching Moon,
my heart has found the one.
With words of charm, and airs mystique,
May mesmerizing words I seek,
Flow freely off my tongue.

Bringing Love

You cannot control another's will with your love spell, but you can send them a love note via the Universe's energies, or open the pathways to your heart to receive love. It will be felt as a subconscious hug, strengthening the connection you have. The Full Moon is a perfect time to invite the energy of abundant love into your heart and connect to that special someone.

Gather a piece of red construction paper, scissors, a black or gold indelible pen, a piece of rose quartz or ruby, matches, a flameproof bowl, and a red rose. A picture of your intended is optional.

1. Place the items on a heatproof surface, making an altar.

2. Cut out a heart shape from the red paper—any size you like.

3. Write the name of your beloved in the center of the heart and draw three lines underneath it.

4. Fold the heart in half along the center line and write your name on each half, on the outside of the heart, surrounding your intended with loving energy.

5. Holding the paper heart and chosen crystal to your heart, take a moment to visualize your love. When ready, say quietly or aloud:

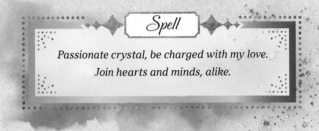

Spell

Passionate crystal, be charged with my love.
Join hearts and minds, alike.

6. Place the paper heart in the bowl and light it with the matches. Imagine the flames igniting love and desire in your intended, carrying your message through the cosmos.

7. Extinguish the flame and take a minute to hold the crystal and feel its loving vibration.

8. Place the rose in a vase by your bed and the crystal under your pillow. Repeat the spell and dream of your love.

Aura of Enchantment

To make yourself irresistible to that certain someone, send out
an aura of enchantment. Let yourself exude mystery, allure, and
spellbinding beauty. Call your goddess allies to channel their
enchanting ways. Ask the Muses to accompany you as you say
quietly or aloud to your desired partner:

Spell

*With face to tempt and words to woo,
enchantment has its eyes on you.
For in my spell you will remain, enraptured
so with love's refrain.
This goddess aura flows from me
and binds us for eternity.
Resist no more my true desire—
surrender to love's growing fire.*

Bergamot Love Spell

Sometimes sharing laughs and thoughts over a drink is the best way to start a budding romance, and it doesn't hurt to brew some herbal magic in your favor! Bergamot's sweet message is one of irresistibility. It beckons love, purification, and protection. Use dried leaves for herbal infusions that may be helpful in meditation. Inhale the fragrance and exhale its sweet scent imbued with your intentions. For love spells, burn a red candle while drinking the tea. Gather the flowers into a bath sachet and surrender your tensions to the soothing water and calming energies of this herb.

Spell

With each warm sip I seek to see beyond the worldly realm.
To understand the joy at hand when those we seek to shun
give us their hand, their hearts, their stand to join us all as one.

Drawing Someone
Special to You

If you want to gain the attentions of someone who's caught your eye to see if sparks may fly, use this bewitching spell.

> **You will need:**
>
> ◆ Two rosebuds
> ◆ Large plate and paper towels
> ◆ Microwave
> ◆ Glass dish or sachet bag
> ◆ Small piece of rose quartz or garnet
> ◆ Drop or two of rose essential oil, optional

1. Line a large plate with paper towels and lay out the rosebuds and petals, mixing them together so you don't know which bud is which. Cover the petals with another paper towel and microwave on High for 2 minutes. Keep an eye on them. Turn the petals over and re-cover. Microwave for 1 minute longer. If they are not completely dried, microwave in 15- to 30-second intervals, checking after each one, until dried.

2. Put the dried petals in a glass dish or sachet bag and add a small piece of rose quartz or garnet, then a drop or two of rose essential oil, if you wish.

3. Place the dish under the Full Moon's light. Take a moment to picture your chosen one. When ready, say quietly or aloud:

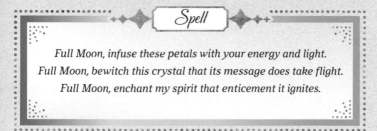

Spell

Full Moon, infuse these petals with your energy and light.
Full Moon, bewitch this crystal that its message does take flight.
Full Moon, enchant my spirit that enticement it ignites.

Take a moment to thank the Moon and imagine your sparks flying out into the Universe. Keep the petals out where you can see them and repeat the spell as desired.

Invoking the Goddesses of Love and Beauty

Invoking the power of the Goddesses of Love and Beauty can be accomplished by setting up an altar and presenting offerings to the Goddess from whom you want to evoke the feelings of love. Here, we call on Freya and Venus.

Make an Offering to Freya

Seek Freya's inspiration when charting your course and stand tall in honor of who you are. Invoke Freya in all your spell work, as she is an eager teacher and will guide your ways. Her mastery of magic, which she taught freely, included the ability to influence the fate and fortunes of others, for which she was enormously respected. Her independent spirit helped her carve her own path.

Offerings

Jewelry, especially amber, is a welcome gift to Freya, as are honey, flowers—especially roses—strawberries, and all things cat-related. Travel-related items, such as maps, and feathers to adorn her altar are favored as well. Using Rune tiles to engage Freya, is also a fun idea.

Make an Offering to Venus

Call upon Venus when your desire is to ignite or rekindle passionate love in your relationship, or to nurture your burning inner passion. Emulate her sensuality and charm. Seek her guidance on looking your best and her confidence to reveal your enchanting beauty to the world to attract what you desire.

Venus, through time, has been goddess of many things, but passion for love and the ability to attract lovers is what she is most celebrated for. She has power over Nature and shines as the brightest star in the sky. Born from the sea, she is also a revered protector of sailors. Her powers of charm and seduction are the stuff of legends.

Offerings

As a goddess of great beauty, Venus will be pleased with gorgeous fresh flowers, especially roses. Other meaningful offerings are seashells, seasonal fruits, honey, and anything red—the color of passionate love—such as red candles or garnets. Keeping her altar tended will keep Venus's fire alive in your soul.

Spell

When beauty floats upon the air, we recognize its scent...
for love ensues, each breath we take, a gift that's goddess-sent.
Unable to resist your face, my goddess of delight,
you sing of beauty all around—reflecting hope and light.
When passions stir and romance blooms, don't hesitate to fall
straight in the arms of goddess love—her beauty beckons all.

Vow of Commitment

Goddesses with the most successful unions stay true to themselves while also committing to the good of all. If commitment is in your future, turn to your favorite goddess for advice on living your true self in a way that benefits you and your current or potential partner.

- ♦ Gather 3 items that symbolize commitment to you and place them on your altar.
- ♦ Create a bouquet of dalias, the flower symbolizing commitment and discovery.
- ♦ Place the bouquet in a vase or tie with a red ribbon and place on your altar.

Once your altar is set, say quietly or aloud:

Spell

O Goddess Realm of unions blessed,
please turn your thoughts my way.
Commitment comes in many forms
and with your help I pray,
that giving love and keeping vows
are sacred in their ways,
of joining two, then, into one,
while each still has a say.

Jasmine Love Oil

Commonly associated with love, sensuality, and prosperity, there's a lot to love about jasmine. It's known for its fragrance, its taste in tea, and its magical properties. When looking for deep, spiritual love, jasmine is the herb to reach for. Combined with a carrier oil, it serves many uses. You can anoint your candles with it, anoint yourself (your hair or your skin), or add a few drops to your bath or sachets. In order to make jasmine oil, you'll need:

♦ A vial or any other small container
♦ Dried jasmine
♦ A carrier oil like almond, jojoba, olive, or grapeseed

Consecutively, add two parts oil and one part jasmine to your container. As you do so, recite this spell quietly or aloud:

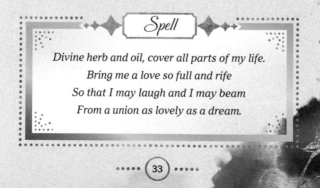

Spell

Divine herb and oil, cover all parts of my life.
Bring me a love so full and rife
So that I may laugh and I may beam
From a union as lovely as a dream.

Confidence Meditation Spell

When finding love is met with adversity, it's very easy to assume you're the problem. That line of thinking is not only false, but damaging! You have many positive qualities, you just need the right person to see them. With this meditation, you will amplify them and strengthen your confidence aura.

On a Friday, the day that represents love, take a moment to meditate. Cleanse your space with sage or incense and clear all clutter. If beneficial, listen to music that will help clear your mind. Write down all your positive qualities, especially anything you've been told by others. When you're finished, read the list over and over until you have it memorized. Then, close your eyes and meditate on those qualities, affirming them in yourself. Keep going until you feel a warmth in your heart, as if you're glowing. Then say:

Spell

I am the good others see in me.
I am the good I see in myself.
I accept me for who I am.
I call for another to do the same.

Love Sigil

In magic, signs and symbols are everything. We look for signs of coincidence, fortune, success, and in this case, love. What's fantastic about love is that it looks different for everyone; the same applies to sigils. No two are alike. Your symbol is unique to you and the love you hope to attract. Sigils are easy magic that anyone can do no matter where you are. All you need is:

- ◆ An indelible or consecrated pen
- ◆ A small piece of paper

To create a sigil:

1. Write out a phrase describing your desire. It can be as simple as "love," or as specific as "a fulfilling relationship."

2. Take your phrase and remove all vowels, then all double consonants.

3. With the remaining letters, soften the focus on your eyes and then loosely trace what the letters look like.

4. Once you have your form down, write more confidently and add swirls or hearts or anything that comes to you.

5. Touch the sigil and imagine your initial phrase. Focus on it, then funnel your emotion into the sigil. Imagine light shining from you onto the symbol.

6. When you're done, you can burn the sigil, add it to charm bags, use it in spell work, or sew it onto sachets. You've just created a physical manifestation of your desire. Use it with care.

Candle Coating Blend

The flame and light of a candle can bring about a sense of calm, which is why they're so often used in our craft. If you want to boost your candles for a quick spell or add some extra power to a long-form ritual, this herbal candle coating is the perfect addition to any love spell work. By combining multiple elements to your candles, you're giving them life and your love more power.

You'll need:

♦ A pink or red chime candle for either love or a combination of love and passion
♦ Mortar and pestle
♦ Jasmine for spiritual love
♦ Dried rose for love and purification (so that your love is always pure)
♦ Sugar so your love is sweet
♦ Dried orange peel for truth
♦ Anointing oil (any carrier oil or the Jasmine Love Oil (see page 33)
♦ A large fireproof container to catch falling herbs
♦ Greaseproof paper or a dish larger than the candle

To coat the candles:

1. Grind the herbs into a fine powder.

2. Take your oil and wipe it over the candle from top to bottom, until completely covered.

3. Lay out the herbs on either the paper or dish.

4. Roll the candle on the herbs, making sure they stick.

5. Put the candle into the fireproof container and light it with a long-stemmed lighter.

Tarot Love Spell

Finding love can be as mysterious as the messages from our tarot cards. Using this divination tool can be exciting because we never know what message the cards may have in store. In this ritual, you will use their powerful messages for your specific purpose. To perform this spell, you must have a loving relationship with yourself and be able to allow your preconceived notions of love and romance to be shaken.

You'll need:

- Two pink candles
  - One for honoring your self-love
  - Another to represent your future relationship
- Jasmine Love Oil for the candles (see page 33)
- A picture of yourself (or something that represents you)
- The Lovers card to represent the love you'll attain
- The Tower card to represent being radically challenged by love
- Moonstone for your inner goddess
- Romantic music to get you in the right mindset
- Three rose quartz pieces to represent love (three for manifestation, but you may use one if needed)

To enact the spell:

1. Anoint the candles.

2. Set them on either end of your altar and light them.

3. Take the object that represents you and The Lovers card and place them in front of their respective candles.

4. Place The Tower card in between the two candles.

5. Place the moonstone underneath The Tower.

6. Touch the moonstone and thank the Moon for blessing the ritual.

7. Play the music while holding on to the rose quartz and whisper words into them:

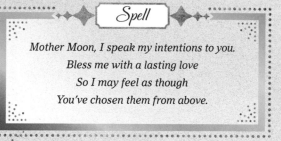

Spell

Mother Moon, I speak my intentions to you.
Bless me with a lasting love
So I may feel as though
You've chosen them from above.

8. Once your emotion is high, place the quartz near your object, then move them over to The Lovers card.

9. Imagine pulling the essence of your object with your hands and then placing it onto The Lovers.

10. From there, hover your hands over the crystals, powering them once more with your intention, then release the energy and lift it to the Moon.

Fictional Romance Spell

Many of us get our first ideas about romance through movies, TV, or books. Though that love isn't always realistic, there's a reason we're attracted to it: the depictions are of a powerful, overwhelming, and seemingly perfect love. This spell will encourage you to look deeper than the shiny exterior of love in the media. Instead of focusing on the aesthetic, focus on what you love about your favorite fictional couple, whether it be their chemistry, compatibility, or friendship.

What you'll need for this spell is:

♦ A piece of paper
♦ An indelible or consecrated pen
♦ A picture of your ideal couple (optional)
♦ Matches
♦ A fireproof container

Now that you've gathered your tools:

1. Write down everything you love about your fictional couple, how they make you feel, what you like about them as characters, anything you can think of. Don't hold back.

2. Next, narrow the list down to what you want for yourself and your future partner.

3. Once you've done so, take the list and say a prayer to Freya:

Spell

This is the love I desire,
The love of my dreams.
I take them to this fire
To fulfill my wants and needs.

4. Light your match and burn the letter, letting it drop into the fireproof container.

5. As an option, you can keep the picture of your ideal couple in your bag or car as a lucky charm.

Seven-day Altar Spell

The search for love is a long process. It doesn't happen in a day; most good things don't. If your efforts haven't been sufficient, you can make a separate altar for love. Dedicated altars, aside from your main altar, are a form of extended-release magic. Because of the concentration of magical items, they're very powerful, making the spells last longer. Passing by the altar every day will remind you of what you want and reassure you that you'll receive it.

For this spell gather:

- ◆ Red or pink cloth as the base of the altar
- ◆ A small bouquet of red roses in a vase as an offering to Venus
- ◆ Juniper for purpose and direction
- ◆ Alfalfa for manifestation
- ◆ Lavender for clarity
- ◆ Watermelon tourmaline for joy and rejuvenation
- ◆ Rose quartz for love and tenderness
- ◆ Moonstone for healing
- ◆ Green aventurine for luck

For this spell, you'll start on Friday, the day of love associated with Venus. Place the cloth on your altar. If possible, use one that'll cover it entirely. Then place the bouquet on the altar while saying a prayer to Venus, thanking her in advance for her help. Over the next six days, place the items before the altar in the order listed. On the seventh day, your altar is complete. Leave it be for a Moon cycle, checking in on the roses occasionally.

2

Long-Term Love

BUILDING A LASTING CONNECTION can take work, a bit of romance, confidence, and trust. Sustainable relationships can grow and blossom into a lifelong partnership. This chapter will give you the spells and rituals to strengthen and improve your long-term love.

The key to lasting love is consistency and keeping close track of how it's growing and developing. In the following pages, you'll become aware of a slew of different ways to keep your mature love going by learning the language of herbs and flowers and how they correspond to love. Some flowers, like roses, are classic symbols of love, but so are cardamom and white flowers, depending on the deity. Others, like snapdragon and cornflower, can be used in weddings and as a crown to bestow on your partner's head.

You've probably heard the common phrase, "spice things up." In witchcraft, we mean it! Spices like cinnamon, jasmine, and rosemary all have love properties and accompany quite a few spells, including potions, baths, charm bags, and more. It just goes to show how powerful they can be!

We also acknowledge the power of crystals. They're perfect for lasting love because they naturally emit frequencies and vibrations that help us in our everyday lives, especially in love. Not only that, they have symbolic meaning, which adds to their resplendency. When it comes to long-term love, crystals—like rose quartz, diamonds, or aventurine—can bring about luck in love and everlasting love. You'll be able to use crystals corresponding with your chakras to promote your health and to prepare you to be a better partner.

Cardamom Herbal Love Spell

Cardamom soothes your thoughts with its warming properties and enchanting aroma. Cardamom instills faithful love, lures lust, and brings on a sweetness of temperament. It calms the mind and clears the cobwebs.

Steep seeds in mulled wine and offer a glass of this aphrodisiac potion to your lover—be forewarned of its power. Diffuse the essential oil to brighten your mood and clear your thoughts. Allow yourself a moment of self-care, sipping a calming cup of chai and closing your eyes, even if only for a moment, to savor the quiet. When ready to cast your spell, say quietly or aloud:

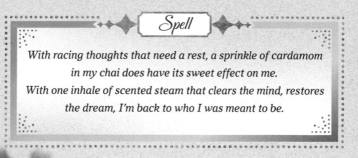

Spell

With racing thoughts that need a rest, a sprinkle of cardamom
in my chai does have its sweet effect on me.
With one inhale of scented steam that clears the mind, restores
the dream, I'm back to who I was meant to be.

Rose Quartz

Rose quartz is the stone of unconditional love—for yourself and others. Good vibes attract good vibes. Rose quartz is best used during the Waning Gibbous phase, fostering feelings of love and gratitude as the Moon's cycle comes to a close.

Carry a rose quartz with you and use it to channel the Moon's loving energy any time you need it. For an extra boost, say quietly or aloud:

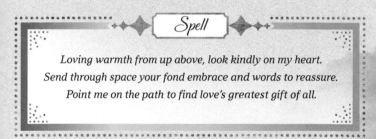

Spell

Loving warmth from up above, look kindly on my heart.
Send through space your fond embrace and words to reassure.
Point me on the path to find love's greatest gift of all.

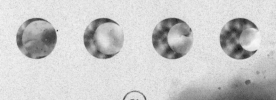

Sugar Scrub
for Sweet Love

Whether you prefer a sweet-smelling lotion or homemade sugar scrub, draw some attention your way. Liberally apply the potion and watch the bees swarm—with a little boost from this spell.

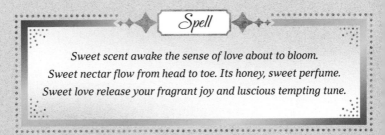

Spell

Sweet scent awake the sense of love about to bloom.

Sweet nectar flow from head to toe. Its honey, sweet perfume.

Sweet love release your fragrant joy and luscious tempting tune.

Everlasting Diamond Spell

The diamond is a symbol of everlasting love and is also believed to instill courage (makes sense, those two go together). However, a diamond worn for effect or prestige will bring the opposite in love.

Hold a diamond and say quietly or aloud:

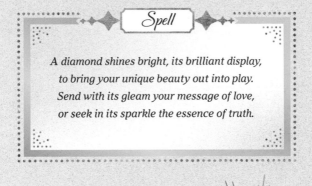

Spell

A diamond shines bright, its brilliant display,
to bring your unique beauty out into play.
Send with its gleam your message of love,
or seek in its sparkle the essence of truth.

Marriage Proposal Spell

A Full Moon can bring out the full depth of love in us. If a proposal is on your mind and you'd like to hurry it along, try pleading your case to the Moon. You can also try this if you're gathering the nerve to make that proposal. Say quietly or aloud:

Spell

Sparkling Moondust glitters and glows,
while magical Moonlight tickles my toes.
Happy and loved I feel when with you.
If married we be, I know we will grow
From one into two, and more may there be,
to bask in our love as a new family.

Cinnamon Herbal Love Spell

Long-lasting love should feel comfortable, peaceful, and serene for both lovers. Cinnamon is the spice of generosity—what's mine is yours. A warming culinary spice, it brings feelings of comfort, coziness, love, and safety. Cinnamon increases spirituality and breeds abundance, power, and success. It also inspires love and lust, and offers protection.

With its association to fire, add cinnamon to any spell to help it manifest more quickly. Cinnamon in potpourri is a lovely way to add soothing fragrance and its magical energies to a room. Hang a cinnamon broom over the main doorway to your home for protective energy and burn cinnamon incense to ignite romance.

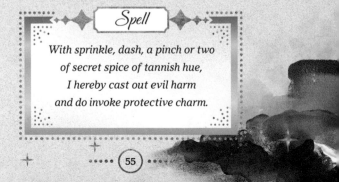

Spell

*With sprinkle, dash, a pinch or two
of secret spice of tannish hue,
I hereby cast out evil harm
and do invoke protective charm.*

Ruby Red Love

A ruby's red color symbolizes love and passion. This stone's glorious color promotes energy, sensuality, and vitality. Hold a ruby and say quietly or aloud:

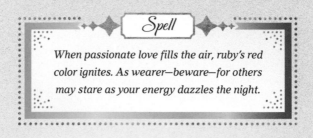

Spell

When passionate love fills the air, ruby's red color ignites. As wearer—beware—for others may stare as your energy dazzles the night.

Rose Herbal Love Spell

Receiving a rose from the one you love is a classic symbol of true and deep devotion. As a gift of joy and promoter of gratitude, roses benefit both the recipient and the giver. It inspires confidence, deepens divination and dreams, ignites love, and brings luck, happiness, and trust.

Scatter rose buds or petals on top of your bed for a sure bet to enhance romance. Relax into a soothing cup of rose petal tea and emerge renewed and refreshed. Add rosewater to a bath and prepare to be seduced. Add petals to a dream sachet and tuck under your pillow for especially prophetic dreams. Sprinkle rose petals on your altar to protect your sacred space. Select three roses and hold them over your heart. Say quietly or aloud:

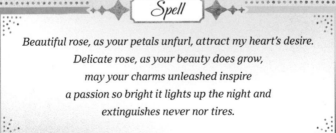

Spell

Beautiful rose, as your petals unfurl, attract my heart's desire.
Delicate rose, as your beauty does grow,
may your charms unleashed inspire
a passion so bright it lights up the night and
extinguishes never nor tires.

Make an Offering to Rhiannon

Call on Rhiannon for matters of domestic happiness, when patience seems elusive and strength beyond your means is needed to reach your goals. Rhiannon demonstrates great strength—physical, spiritual, and mental—in the face of significant challenges and patience in awaiting the redemption of truth. Her beauty and powers of courage are great sources of inspiration. She has the power to reveal truth in dreams.

Offerings

Anything related to horses or birds will delight Rhiannon. Consider also safely burning white candles or place white flowers in a vase, a moonstone, or a gift on your altar in gratitude to the people in your life who sustain you.

Spell

As goddess rides across the sky, as Sun, or Moon,
or rainbow high, so signaled here on Earth am I:
To open ears and mind and eyes
to notice what the heart doth spy;
to hear a loved one's precious sigh
or dream of that which beckons nigh.
To see what's right before my eyes,
to choose the truth above a lie.
To seek forgiveness, just and true,
and offer it in kind to you.
O goddess, draw this precious veil,
that worlds unknown revealed do hail.

Burning Love Ritual

When you need to fan the dying embers in a relationship, slip into a warm bath scattered with rose petals—placing some under your pillow can help, too.

What you'll need:

- Red candle
- Rose quartz crystals or garnets, for love
- 15 drops rose essential oil
- Rose petals or a rose

1. Fill your tub with soothing warm water.

2. Place the candle on a sturdy surface. Place the crystals around the candle to cast your circle. Light the candle.

3. Pour the essential oil mix into the tub and swirl it around with your hand to distribute. Be aware of the sensation of the water—feel the fluid caress and softness.

4. Scatter the rose petals onto the water's surface and let their loving symbolism infuse the water. Imagine the water is about to embrace you like a lover.

5. Slip into the bath and relax into the sensual feel of the water. Gaze softly into the candle's flame as you feel your energy rise. Take a moment in silent gratitude for the life-giving water and the opportunity for self-care.

6. Invite your goddess into your circle. Close your eyes and, when ready, say quietly or aloud:

Spell

Such beauty as yours ignites flames of desire.
I seek to touch your soul with mine
to light my flame within.
Venus [or goddess of choice],
grant me your smoldering passion
that burns without end to excite.
A lesson in charm meant to tempt without
harm can transform me as day into night.
With petals as soft as my lover's sweet kiss,
I place roses as thanks at your feet.
In fire as bright as your burning delight,
I see my lover awaiting tonight.

Long Live Love!

When you find that special someone, love seems so easy. As it ages, though, it does take more work to keep it alive. It ebbs and flows and changes and grows, just like the seasons. Learning to go with the flow is key to making love last. It is something to be worshipped and celebrated in its own right. Take wisdom from any goddess of love you trust and say quietly or aloud, as often as you like, to conjure a lifetime of love that holds up to anything:

Spell

When love chooses you, all the world seems anew.
Dear goddess, please grant me this wish:
May what's new today weather well and
turn gray as the fires of passion do die,
but smoldering still have the heat to sustain
through both good times and darkness of night.
When life's reached its end, my prayer is that, then,
our love still shines blindingly bright.

Lasting Love Sachet

Sachets are powerful tools you can use to strengthen an already solid relationship. Your unique sachet contains all the magic you need to keep you mindful of your intentions and make you feel more committed and aware of your connection to your partner.

You'll use:

◆ A small pouch with a drawstring
◆ Rice for abundance
◆ A note with your intentions
◆ Clear quartz for enhancement
◆ Garnet for mutual love
◆ A small item that represents you and your significant other
◆ Body spray, cologne, or perfume
◆ Pens or needle and thread to draw the rune symbol (optional)

Fill the bag halfway with rice. Add in a note with your wish
for the relationship so it's at the center of the sachet. Add both
crystals and the small item and top the bag off with rice. Last,
spray with a scent that will make you think of your beloved.
If you like, you can embroider or draw the rune symbol for
Kenaz on top of the bag. Kenaz stands for sexual energy,
transformation, passion, and strength.

Place your sachet in the area where you and your significant
other spend the most time together, like underneath the pillows
of your bed or under the couch pillows in the living room.

Vision Board Spell

As with anything in life that we desire, it's essential to define our goals so that we can work actively toward them. In love, it can mean you're in a relationship and you want to see which direction you want it to go and, ultimately, what you want from it. You can't rush love, but you can define what you want to get out of it. This vision board is for when you don't have the words to express your desires, so you let your creativity take over. Make the message as clear as you can so that when you look at it, you'll instantly be reminded of your intentions.

If you have it, grab some turmeric from your spice cabinet and have a taste. Turmeric is a spice of creativity and energy. To begin your board, you'll need a canvas. This can be something as big as poster board or as small as cardstock. Because this is a creative project, you'll need a medium like pens, markers, or paints. Combine colors, make sigils, write your intentions—anything that gets your message across. Lastly, add the finishing touches with glitter glue, pictures, or washi tape stickers. Once you're done, place your board somewhere you're going to see it every day, so your intentions are clear, and you don't settle for less.

Love Tincture

Tinctures, made from alcohol and herbs, are some of the most potent forms of potions. The alcohol draws out the extracts of each herb you place in with it to produce a commanding aphrodisiac. You can add tinctures to water or tea for a light effect, or take a drop or two straight up.

This love tincture is meant to calm the nerves and remove any inhibition that might separate you from your beloved. When taken with your intended, it can put you both in a calmer, more open state of mind where love, romance, or bedroom play can occur.

To make the tincture, you'll need:

♦ Orange peel for passion
♦ Chamomile for bliss
♦ Lavender for taste and smell
♦ Dried rose for protection so that you feel safe
♦ Jasmine for relaxation and sexual desire
♦ A glass jar
♦ 80 proof vodka (preferred), rum, or grain alcohol
♦ Strainer (or cheesecloth), to strain

Add the orange peel, herbs, and flowers to the glass jar so that they make up half of the jar's contents. As you add each new ingredient, say aloud or in your head, *May this bring about love*, then pour in your chosen alcohol. Make sure the herbs are completely submerged. Close the lid of the jar; if the lid is made of metal, be sure to use parchment paper as a buffer between the two. Let the mixture sit in a cool place for one Moon cycle. Every few days, check to make sure the alcohol hasn't evaporated. Give it a few shakes periodically.

When the Moon cycle is up, use the strainer to strain your tincture, then transfer it to a clean jar or bottle that has an eyedropper lid. Discard the herbs.

Cozy Love Potion

One of the challenges of long-term love is maintaining vulnerability with another person. Being open about how much you care for someone or being unsure of how they feel about you can make you want to hide your emotions or keep your guard up. Love thrives with openness and transparency, and this calming potion can help you be just that.

Instead of being caught up with what you should say to the other person or how they'll take it, you can use a diffuser so that love will literally be in the air. Once you smell the scents of your magic, you'll be calmed and soothed enough to be unguarded.

Gather:

♦ Charged (or Moon water) water as the base
♦ Your cauldron (or any other bowl)
♦ Pink salt for romance
♦ Lavender essential oil for peace and calm
♦ Orange essential oil for confidence and growth
♦ Rose for protection
♦ Chamomile for abundance
♦ A diffuser

Prepare this mixture three hours ahead of when you'll see your beloved—ideally leading into the evening. The darker the day, the more open people become.

Take your charged water and pour it into your cauldron. Then, add in the salt and stir to help the dissolving process. Add three drops of each oil and the floral ingredients. Stir the mixture again, slowly, and as you do so, whisper:

Spell

May this make me brave enough
to express my feelings,
open enough to invite love in,
and safe enough to share my heart.

Set the mixture on your windowsill (preferably one facing the Moon) and let sit for three hours. Add the mixture to your diffuser and place it somewhere you can smell it. As you're cozying up to your person, let the scents calm and guide you.

Domestic Love Powder

Your home is your haven. It's where you eat, sleep, and share memories with those important to you. Because home is such an essential part of your life, it should always be filled with love. This domestic love powder has many uses—including seasoning your food, blessing your altar, adding to your bath, coating your candles, or sprinkling it about your house. No matter how you use it, it will elevate and maintain a feeling of love throughout your practice and your home.

You will need:

- Freeze-dried strawberries for dedication
- Cinnamon for vivacity
- Nutmeg for strength
- Rosemary for love and loyalty
- Dried hibiscus for lust
- 3 drops of lavender essential oil to promote feelings of love
- A jar (preferably red or pink)
- Mortar and pestle

Grind each herb one by one, turning the pestle clockwise in the mortar, while humming your favorite love song. Songs tend to stick with us and carry certain feelings and memories. You'll want all those good vibes to go into the herbs. Place the herbs into the jar in thirds. With each third, put in one drop of the lavender oil.

Once you're finished, shake the jar three times in one hand and three times in the other. Then hold the jar in your hands, enclosing it tight, and think of everything you love about your relationship. Let the feelings build like air filling a balloon, and once it pops, imagine that love raining down on the jar.

Grateful for Love Ritual

Love is such a beautiful and powerful emotion. It can be uplifting, energizing, and life-changing, so it's good to be grateful for it when you have it. Long-lasting love comes not only with time but with gratitude. Appreciating your partner for who they are and what they bring to the relationship not only promotes intimacy, it also fosters affection. Giving thanks to Mother Moon acknowledges how she's helped you along and is a way to feed more love into your union.

What you'll need:

♦ A red candle for deep love
♦ A gold (or yellow) candle for happiness
♦ A silver candle to represent the Moon
♦ Green aventurine for love and luck
♦ A photo of you and your significant other
♦ Sugar to taste and to extract positive energies

Perform this ritual right before a Full Moon. This is the time to reflect and look back on the Moon cycle and your love life so far. If possible, before performing the spell, have your loved one touch the aventurine crystal and obtain a photo of them. This will impart some of their energy. During the ritual, light the candles and place the aventurine on top of the picture. Place your fingers on the crystals and focus on what makes your relationship special, what you have now that you've never had before, and how lucky you are to have found each other. Then say this prayer:

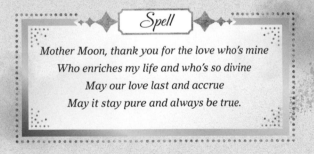

Spell

Mother Moon, thank you for the love who's mine
Who enriches my life and who's so divine
May our love last and accrue
May it stay pure and always be true.

Have a small taste of the sugar to end the ritual on a sweet note. Find your beloved and tell them how grateful you are to have them.

Dreamy Romance Bath

Nothing beats a bath with your lover. Relaxing and intimate, it can be the setup for an erotic evening. If you want to beguile your beloved, this bath will have them feeling warm, content, appreciated, and in a romantic mood. Perform this ritual during the Waxing Moon as a buildup to this special moment.

For this bath, you'll need:

- Dried orange peel for truth
- Dried jasmine for spiritual love
- Dried catnip for happiness
- A mortar and pestle
- A muslin bag
- White candles to represent all that love can bring
- Pink candles for love
- Rose quartz crystals
- Lavender Epsom salts for peace and relaxation
- Fresh pink petals for aesthetics and smell
- Fresh passion flowers for passion

Start filling the tub with water, setting it to the perfect temperature. Gather your dried ingredients and roughly crush them using the mortar and pestle to release their fragrance, but not so much that they become a fine powder. Place them in the muslin bag and let them soak in the water in the tub for a while. Next, take the candles and place them around your bathroom where they'll be out of the way of anything that can catch fire. If possible, line some of them on the tub's edge. Pair them with some rose quartz and place one crystal in the tub itself.

Pour the Epsom salts into the water and stir with your hand to imbue the water with some of your energy. Lastly, as the water rises to your desired height, sprinkle the rose petals and place the passion flowers on the surface while reciting this prayer.

Spell

Loving herbs, open our hearts and relax our minds
So that we can slow down and take our time
Being present, being together
Creating a moment we can treasure.

Allure Potion

Most magic is in the mind, but this magic is in the gut. Love potions have been around as long as magic has. There's always the desire to make someone love you, but this potion will make your lover want you. Romantic love is dreamy and can be wistful, but for it to be well-rounded, there needs to be room for lust and play. If you find your sex life is a little lacking, this alluring potion will put you and your beloved under your spell, readying you to enjoy where the night goes.

Gather:

♦ Dried hibiscus for passion
♦ Dried rose petals for love
♦ Cinnamon for energy
♦ Nutmeg to enhance the cinnamon
♦ Honey for sweetness and sensuality
♦ A dash of turmeric for lust
♦ Love Tincture (see page 66)
♦ Fancy cups or goblets
♦ Candles and incense, optional

For this spell, gather the ingredients during the Waxing Moon to build tension with the intention to make the potion during the Full Moon. Flirt with and romance your partner in small ways throughout the gathering process to lay the foundation with them.

Place the dried herbs in a steeper. Boil some water as the base for the tea potion. Steep the herbs for ten minutes in the boiling water. Scoop them out and discard them. With a stirrer or small wooden spoon, stir the infused tea. Then add in the cinnamon, honey, and turmeric, pausing to taste after each addition. Add three to five drops of the love tincture and stir for the final time. Say quietly or aloud:

Spell

Potion of love and lust,
help me pull them in and gain their trust
so I may sway and entice my love on this night.

Pour some of the mixture for you and your love into fancy cups or goblets, set the mood with candles or incense, and serve.

Loving Flower Crown

People in love may often call their partner their "king" or "queen." Love is so rich; it can feel like your intended rules your heart. So, what better way to honor your significant other than crowning them as yours for all to see?

Flower crowns have a centuries-long history of being used during wedding ceremonies, signifying unity and fertility. If you intend for your partner to be your forevermore, bestow this crown on them to show them how much they mean to you. You'll make them feel like the royalty they are.

You'll need:

- Wire for the headband
- Tape measure
- Floral tape
- Scissors
- Cornflower for inviting love in
- Lavender for love and happiness
- Daffodil for high vibrations
- Snapdragon for protection
- Your beau's favorite flower
- Craft wire to tie the flowers to the crown

Take the wire and measure your beloved's head to make sure it fits but isn't too snug. You'll need a bit of extra room for the flowers. If this crown is a surprise, use a hat they've worn and measure the wire with that, adding about half an inch. Close the wire with floral tape and cut the excess wire. Next, you'll have to create small clusters of flowers. Trim each flower and arrange them like a bouquet around the wire crown. When you get them how you want them, use the floral tape to keep them together, then wrap the craft wire around the small bouquets to secure them to the crown.

As you wrap and place each flower or bundle, personally thank each for its properties and for being a part of this token of love. You can either give this to your beloved right away or put it in the fridge to keep it fresh until the time is right. When the flowers wilt, bury them in the ground, so you return nature to nature.

Chakra Crystal Necklace

For love to last, the body's needs must come first. When our chakras are blocked or not functioning correctly, they affect our lives. We can become overly anxious, doubtful, or cold. A healthy love requires each party to be open with what they want (sacral chakra), how they feel (heart chakra), and what they want to say (throat chakra). If those areas aren't in order, love suffers. This chakra crystal necklace will be a constant reminder to keep those areas open so that you, and your relationship, will thrive.

What you'll need:

♦ Sacral Chakra—carnelian chips for your deepest desires
♦ Heart Chakra—emerald chips for enhancing unconditional love and unity
♦ Throat Chakra—blue lace agate chips for articulation
♦ A small glass vial with a cork
♦ Incense
♦ A small hook eye
♦ Hot glue gun and glue
♦ A chain or leather strap for the necklace

Before crafting the necklace, make sure you cleanse and charge the crystals under the moonlight. This will clear them of any other use and give them the energy they need to help you. To cleanse the jar, light some incense, stick it inside the jar, then shake it until the jar becomes opaque. Hold each set of crystal chips onto their corresponding chakra area of your body. Bring each cluster near your mouth and speak your intention into them. Then, little by little, add the chips to the jar. Take the hook eye and stick it into the cork, adding some glue to it. Take the hot glue gun and carefully trace the lip of the jar. Insert the cork. Thread your necklace of choice through the hook and wear. Recharge every two months.

Poppet Healing Spell

Poppets are a special kind of magic, full of caring connotations. They're a form of sympathetic magic, meaning they represent someone or something. Whatever you do to the poppet happens to the person it represents. One of the best expressions of love is taking care of another person when they're unwell. That's where this poppet comes in.

With the permission of your partner, this poppet will be a great supplement to their care regimen. However, keep in mind it's not a replacement for prescribed or over-the-counter medicine, rather it's supplemental magic. To start, you'll need:

- Carnation plant for longevity
- Echinacea plant for amplification
- Three sticks of birch wood (or maple or oak) for healing and protection
- String (or twine)
- Scissors to cut the string
- Pine sprigs for abundance
- Eucalyptus sprigs for physical healing
- Lavender sprigs for intimate healing

Take both the carnation and echinacea plants and tie them to one stick of birch wood with the string. Don't tie so tightly that you dent the stems of the flowers, but tight enough that they don't move too easily. Do this on both ends. The flowers will represent the head. Next, split the remaining sprigs so that one of each is tied to the remaining two sticks. These represent the arms and legs. Take the arms and legs and tie them to the body horizontally. When finished, gently hold the poppet in your hands and say in your head or aloud:

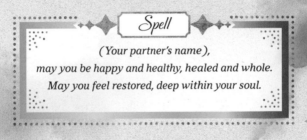

Spell

(Your partner's name),
may you be happy and healthy, healed and whole.
May you feel restored, deep within your soul.

Place the poppet somewhere safe, either close to your beloved or somewhere it can be left in peace. Check in with it from time to time, giving it your love and desire for good health. When your partner is all healed up, take the poppet and bury it in the earth.

3

Relationship
Troubles

RELATIONSHIP TROUBLES CAN SEEM like the worst thing to happen, but they can actually be beneficial. Still, they're never pleasant to go through. The heartache, frustration, and headaches they bring can make relationships difficult when all you want to do is move forward. Thankfully, we don't have to go it alone. We have an array of tools by our side, and this chapter is filled with spells to help you navigate the rougher parts of love.

The goddesses in our lives have lived centuries, and they offer the best advice. Just like anyone who's been in love, they understand that forgiveness, compromise, and a willingness to give love, even when you don't want to, are crucial to mend your relationships. Here, you'll be able to seek their counsel as needed for matters of the heart. And, of course, there's also the beauty of Mother Moon, who can hold you through times of grief and difficulty.

There are so many herbs for love and happiness, but there are also those for heartbreak. Heartache has been around since human existence, so it's no wonder Mother Nature created them just for us. Herbs, like bleeding heart and witch hazel, not only soothe our broken hearts when we need them, but they're protective as well. They can be used to help us attract new love when an old one is gone. When stuffed in a seashell, they can help us let go. There's no end to their power.

Here, you'll rely on yourself as well as your craft to pull you out of sadness and disappointment with both self-love spells and intense shadow work. This is where healing begins.

Forgiveness Ritual

All relationships, in order to thrive, require forgiving and forgiveness. Whether giving or receiving, doing so must be from a true heart. Forgiveness releases pain and makes room for love to grow. With help from your favorite goddess, say quietly or aloud:

Spell

*O goddess whose grace is forgiveness
and whose forgiveness is grace, walk with me.
Forgiveness is hard, whether earned on my own,
or given to others in need.
Show me the path that leads to the well of
those healing waters you speak of,
for there I can drink of the balm that will lead
to the soothing forgiveness I seek.*

Anger Antidote

When anger threatens to take you and your relationship under, stop, take a deep breath, and seek solace in an herbal charm.

♦ Lavender calms, chamomile murmurs soothing scents, and lemon balm clears the mind.
♦ Add Chinese chrysanthemum for cheerfulness in adversity, and Damask rose to refresh your thoughts of self-love.

Make a sachet to carry for unexpected events, or mindfully gather what you can from your garden as you seek to calm the mind. Create an herbal circle around a blue candle. Light the flame and gaze into it until you feel your heartbeat slow. Sip a soothing cup of chrysanthemum tea. Repeat the following as needed:

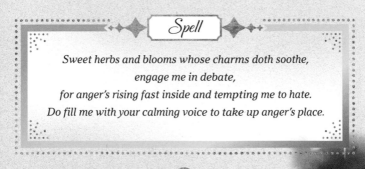

Spell

Sweet herbs and blooms whose charms doth soothe,
engage me in debate,
for anger's rising fast inside and tempting me to hate.
Do fill me with your calming voice to take up anger's place.

Relationship Troubles Ritual

Trouble in your relationship may be something you've been reflecting on and trying to resolve. During the Waning Moon phase, align with the fading energies to slow down and search deep within, to ask yourself what it is you want versus what you have. How can you take steps to make the two meet?

In this time of uncertainty, our self-talk can get negative. Use the Moon's gorgeous glimmer to see your beauty within and out. Try this affirmation when you need a little self-love:

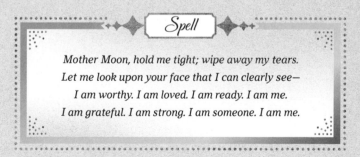

Spell

Mother Moon, hold me tight; wipe away my tears.
Let me look upon your face that I can clearly see—
I am worthy. I am loved. I am ready. I am me.
I am grateful. I am strong. I am someone. I am me.

Take a moment to congratulate yourself for showing up today, as hard as it may be, knowing tomorrow will give you another chance.

Give and Take

Relationships thrive when each person involved is allowed to be an individual as well as a member of the team. Managing conflicting expectations requires give and take, and the flexibility that acceptance and nonjudgment afford. Call on any of the Mother Goddesses for their spirit of unconditional love, to help when the relationship road feels a little rocky, or to remind you why you're in the relationship in the first place. When ready, say quietly or aloud:

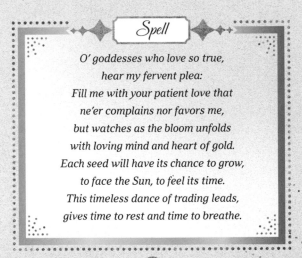

Spell

O' goddesses who love so true,
hear my fervent plea:
Fill me with your patient love that
ne'er complains nor favors me,
but watches as the bloom unfolds
with loving mind and heart of gold.
Each seed will have its chance to grow,
to face the Sun, to feel its time.
This timeless dance of trading leads,
gives time to rest and time to breathe.

Give Love Always Spell

I particularly like the Goddesses Amaterasu and Kuan Yin for this reminder: Do not withhold love—ever. When important relationships leave us feeling hurt or let down, it's easy to withdraw and withhold love as punishment. But you're only punishing yourself and hurting those who love you in the process. While it's not always easy, remember, love begets love. Speak to Amaterasu for help seeing the truth, and Kuan Yin for compassionate wisdom, when pain or anger threatens to draw you inward.

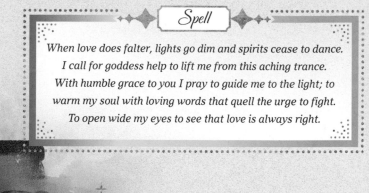

Spell

When love does falter, lights go dim and spirits cease to dance.
I call for goddess help to lift me from this aching trance.
With humble grace to you I pray to guide me to the light; to
warm my soul with loving words that quell the urge to fight.
To open wide my eyes to see that love is always right.

Calling on the Goddess Kali

Kali is an indestructible force in the Hindu religion. Kali, whose original name is Dakshina Kālikā, is the goddess of time, creation, and destruction. She chases and decimates evil, but only for those she loves. Once she's done her work, beauty and creation can begin.

While healing from a breakup, it's tempting to hold on to old habits or ideals from the relationship. They may have served a purpose in the past, but now you need them out so you can start anew. Only invoke Kali if you're ready for your life to drastically change or if you need a clean break from the past. To invoke Kali, display a picture or statue of her on your altar. As you look at her, say:

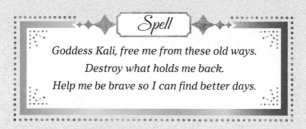

Spell

Goddess Kali, free me from these old ways.
Destroy what holds me back.
Help me be brave so I can find better days.

Bleeding Heart Love Spell

An old-fashioned stalwart of the gardens, bleeding heart speaks freely of emotions . . . of love, of heartbreak, of compassion. In some cultures, it represents the pain of being rejected by a lover, while in others it is offered as a symbol of true love. Bleeding heart can open your heart to unconditional love after loss and ease the pain of a broken heart.

Plant bleeding heart in your garden in memory of a lost loved one—if you must plant it indoors, bury a coin in the pot to short-circuit the negative energies it is said to emit when not allowed to grow freely. Include sprigs in wedding flowers for undying love. Keep the flowers in sight to remind you that no matter the loss, love will bloom again.

Spell

Prepare the ground have I to receive this bleeding heart,
to cradle, raise, and nurture well its blooming true love song.
For when I spy its sweet love charms and hear their winsome tune
my heart responds with joyful verse and hope for new love soon.

LOSS

Loss comes in all forms. When you've experienced a simple loss that just has you a bit out of sorts, take a moment to consider all you *do* have to be grateful for. Write it down if it helps the thoughts stick.

If your loss is greater and you need a hug from the Universe and a little self-love to get you back in action, sprinkle a few drops of rose essential oil on a pink or white candle. Light the candle on a heatproof surface and gaze into the flame, letting it and the oil's scent relax you. When you're ready, invite your favorite domestic goddess, the Earth, Sun, or Moon, to sit with you.

Spell

I light this candle to remind myself that darkness can turn bright.
I light this candle to dispel the stormy mood I fight,
for loss and doubt have turned my will into a frozen plight.
I seek the candle's warmth to thaw the cold that's gripped my heart,
its glow to find that piece of me that's ready to restart.

Letting Go

The beauty of releasing something that no longer serves is in the freedom it provides—from guilt, from worry, from fear, from disappointment. In its place is a wide-open space ready to be filled with intentions that align with our priorities. Crone goddesses, particularly Hecate, can help us see clearly when that time has come. When ready to face the reality, say quietly or aloud:

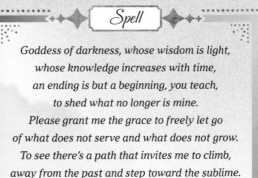

Spell

Goddess of darkness, whose wisdom is light,
whose knowledge increases with time,
an ending is but a beginning, you teach,
to shed what no longer is mine.
Please grant me the grace to freely let go
of what does not serve and what does not grow.
To see there's a path that invites me to climb,
away from the past and step toward the sublime.

Witch Hazel
Herbal Love Spell

Mending a broken heart isn't always easy, but some witch hazel will help heal a soul when love has gone astray. A protector against the evil eye and harmful spirits, witch hazel is also a potent energizer in love spells and a healer of broken hearts. It can restore emotional balance when strong emotions flare.

Instead of smudging, wave a branch or two of witch hazel throughout your home, paying special attention to doorways, closets, corners, and windows, to expel negative energies and evil forces. Plant witch hazel on your property for its protective aura, or keep its flowering branches on your altar and add blooms for a protective charm. Its affinity for finding water, as well as treasure, also makes witch hazel a good companion for weather and money spells.

Spell

The rain is needed desperately to give the Earth a break.
Witch hazel, spread your branches wide and call upon the sky:
Assemble clouds and lightning proud to shed their healing tears
so, when it's done, the Earth's great thirst will fully have been slaked.

Soothing a Broken Heart

Lost love is a special kind of pain—one that, like Nature, must take its own time to heal. To help ease you through the process, any or all of these special herbs can protect and help heal a broken heart. Call on bleeding heart, chives, dill, lavender, and witch hazel. Add rosemary to maintain the happy memories. Put any or all in a tear jar, to catch your tears as they fall. When the jar is full and the tears evaporate, your heart is said to be healed.

Spell

The pain brings life to a halt,
and it matters not who's at fault.
These tears do I weep,
cleanse my soul from down deep,
but seem unwilling to halt.
When combined with these herbs
may my heart feel a surge
of a hope that can signal restart.

Make an Offering to Epione

Call on the goddess Epione to help soothe pain in all its forms. Her presence can be the balm needed to bring calm and usher in true healing. Though not much is known about Epione, her legacy of soothing is reputable and the power of healing is the mission of her family.

Offerings

An altar dedicated to Epione is a powerful presence in a home, and simple offerings of salt and clean water for cleansing, as well as fresh herbs for healing, will help draw her powers to you.

Spell

Goddess, please do share your spell
to dampen swift each fire that swells.
So, buoyed I be by your great charms
that never will my home know harm,
Just joy and bounty far and wide—
each reaped with gratitude and pride.
This home and hearth, dear goddess, bless,
that love and time reveal our best.

Attracting Love Again

Breakups are one of the most challenging things we can go through. It's a loss and can take some time to heal. As much as it hurts, the only way out is through the sadness and the pain. Once you've recovered and you're ready to open your heart again, this spell will help attract love to you.

You will need:

♦ Palo santo (for cleansing smoke)
   or cinnamon stick (as a non-smoking cleanser)
♦ A white candle for balance
♦ A pink candle for harmony
♦ Aventurine for future love
♦ The Ace of Cups Tarot card for a fresh start
♦ An indelible or consecrated pen
♦ A small piece of paper

With everything in place:

1. Cleanse the area with either method.

2. Arrange your altar with the candles, the aventurine, and the Tarot card.

3. Light the candles, then focus on your desire to attract love. Be careful not to picture someone specifically. You're meant to be open to any new love you'll receive.

4. Read this chant three times:

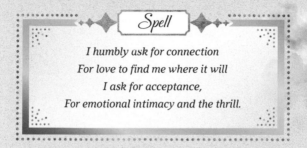

Spell

I humbly ask for connection
For love to find me where it will
I ask for acceptance,
For emotional intimacy and the thrill.

5. Breathe and relax. As you do so, release your intention out to the Universe.

6. Take the pen and piece of paper and write, *Love will come to me.*

7. On your small, arranged altar, place the aventurine atop the Ace of Cups, then place the piece of paper next to that and, lastly, the candles.

8. Let the candles safely burn out and leave the rest of the altar be for a week.

Seashell Release Spell

When a relationship ends, it can be challenging to process. Someone who took up space in your life is now gone. It's normal to focus on all the good things about the relationship. But if your fixation consumes you, it's time to let go and move on. With this spell, you will bind your unresolved thoughts and emotions so you can move forward.

Perform this spell on a Saturday. That's the day associated with Saturn and is perfect for banishing and cutting cords.

The materials you need for this are:

♦ Piece of paper
♦ An indelible or consecrated pen
♦ Bay leaf for writing
♦ Mortar and pestle
♦ Alfalfa for release
♦ Sandalwood for healing
♦ Mint for self-reliance
♦ A conch or shell horn seashell (or any other seashell with a narrow opening)
♦ Black beeswax candle (or coconut wax candle) for banishing
♦ Black cloth to protect the shell

Take a scrap piece of paper and draw your sigil with your pen.
You can even write out a single word if you like. When you're
satisfied, transfer the drawing, or word, over to the bay leaf.
Next, take the mortar and pestle and grind up each herb one by
one. With each new herb, recite this spell to them:

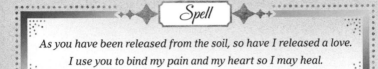

Spell

*As you have been released from the soil, so have I released a love.
I use you to bind my pain and my heart so I may heal.*

Don't grind them so much that they become a powder, but
just enough to release their fragrance and power.

Pour the herbs into the shell and fill it as much as you can.
Light your black candle and let the wax cover the shell's
opening. When you're ready, wrap your shell in black cloth
and take it to the nearest river, lake, or ocean. Wear clothes
that you don't mind getting wet and plan to arrive before or
during sunset. Go as far into the water as you're comfortable
with and lift the shell toward the sky. Quietly say, *I offer this
to you, Saturn, and I leave my past behind me.* Drop or throw the
shell into the water.

Protection from an Ex's Hex

A hex is a "softer" form of a curse. It's an intentional flow of negative energy directed your way. The hexer may not be a witch but instead is someone who has a strong desire for you and your partner's downfall, like a former lover or a jealous friend. These negative energies can wreak havoc in your life and your relationship.

A hex can manifest itself in more arguments, misunderstandings, or increased tension with no discernible reason. If you believe you're being hexed, this spell will allow you to not only return it to the sender but also protect your household from any more harm.

For this, you'll need:

♦ Frankincense incense for cleansing
♦ A small jar
♦ Wormwood for sending back negative energies
♦ Rosemary for fighting evil spirits or intentions
♦ Honeysuckle for peace and freedom
♦ Labradorite for shielding you from ill-will and fixation
♦ Amethyst to amplify the spell's effect
♦ A black candle to seal the jar

- ♦ A portable mirror for reflection
- ♦ A small bundle of devil's shoestring
- ♦ Black salt as a barrier

Light the incense to cleanse your space and the jar. Place the herbs in the jar one at a time, focusing on their intention. Then, hold the crystals in your hand, infusing them with your energy. Enclose them in your fist, close your eyes, and imagine your strong will flowing from your hands into the crystals to charge them. Place them in the jar. Close the lid and then place the black candle on top, light it, and let it coat the jar.

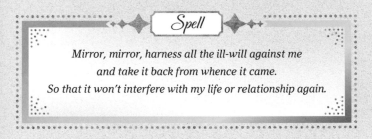

Spell

*Mirror, mirror, harness all the ill-will against me
and take it back from whence it came.
So that it won't interfere with my life or relationship again.*

Leave it on your windowsill until sunrise. Take the jar and your black salt outside to your garden or backyard. Bury the jar so it leaves no bump. Then sprinkle the black salt around your property, imagining there's a shield going up.

Tackling Conflict Tea

No relationship is without its issues, and it's essential to address them as soon as possible. But sometimes even the idea of conflict can send us running for the nearest forest. Conflict is necessary and, at times, unavoidable. As witches, we need to keep our spirits and relationships as free and open as possible. This potion will help to give you and your beloved the bravery to sit down and sort your issues.

Before preparing this spell, make sure you and your significant other have time to have a conversation. You'll want no distractions or anything that will hinder you.

You'll need:

- ♦ Hibiscus for harmony
- ♦ Chamomile for stress reduction
- ♦ Cornflower for happiness
- ♦ Lavender for peace
- ♦ Orange peel for truth
- ♦ Tea steeper
- ♦ One or two drops of the Love Tincture for love (see page 66)
- ♦ Bloodstone for strength

Gather the herbs and orange peel in a steeper, making sure to feel each one before placing them inside. Allow their texture to ground and calm you. Boil some water and pour it in, leaving the herbs to steep for ten minutes in the boiling water. Discard the herbs, then add the Love Tincture. Do this ten minutes before talking to your partner, to let the effects set in. Take a few sips to prepare you, then keep a bloodstone in your pocket for strength. Say a prayer to your patron deity, asking for their guidance. When you're ready, ask your beloved if they'd like tea.

Thyme for Patience

In any union, even the healthy ones, there's going to be frustration. Whether it's because you can't understand your partner or their quirks are driving you up the wall, frustration will rear its head. Irritation stems from impatience, and a lack of patience can cause problems in an otherwise fulfilling relationship.

Thankfully, thyme is the perfect solution for this. It has so many remarkable properties to it. Thyme is a transformative herb that can turn sadness or anger into peace. It's also an energy cleanser, making it ideal for protection spells. In its concentrated oil form, this household herb will help you slow down, take a deep breath, and get to the heart of your exasperation.

What you'll need for this spell:

♦ Charged water
♦ Diffuser
♦ 3 drops of thyme oil for neutralizing anger
♦ 3 drops of lavender essential oil for calm
♦ 3 drops of lemon essential oil for peace
♦ Your journal
♦ An indelible or consecrated pen

Pour your charged water into your diffuser. Though this is more of a reflection spell, you'll want vibrational water to charge the oils and energize your practice. Parse out the drops per oil. Stir with your finger. Place the diffuser near your altar and give it a moment or two to infuse the air. Sit at your altar and take out your journal and pen. Without editing, write why you're frustrated. Say how it makes you feel and what's driving you nuts. Then ask yourself if your partner knows they're frustrating you. Have you told them, or have you been biting your tongue? Contemplate these answers.

Once you're done, close your eyes and take five deep breaths, noting the combined smell of the oils. At the end of the deep breaths, say,

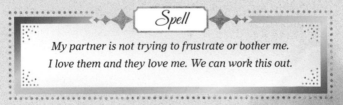

Spell

My partner is not trying to frustrate or bother me.
I love them and they love me. We can work this out.

Repeat as many times as you need.

Have No Doubt

Doubt is a neurological tool that we use to protect ourselves. If we're doubtful the weather is going to be nice, we might not go outside. If we're unsure whether food has expired, we won't eat it. And if a relationship isn't going the way we want it to, we may doubt it's any good for us at all. Past trauma can sow doubt in current relationships, especially healthy ones. If you're used to destructive paths, healthy relationships may feel foreign. The crux of doubt is fear. We, as witches, don't live by fear, but instead by mindfulness. This crystal combination spell will help dissipate your worries and give you a new perspective.

Materials you'll need:

- ◆ Your journal and a piece of paper
- ◆ An indelible or consecrated pen
- ◆ Selenite for cleansing negative energy
- ◆ Amethyst for clarity
- ◆ Chrysoprase for cleansing the heart
- ◆ Rhodochrosite for tender love
- ◆ Malachite for breaking free of negative patterns

In your journal, write a list of all the good things about your lover and what you like about the relationship. Write down as much as you can think of. Then, on a separate piece of paper, write what you're afraid of. What's making you doubtful?

Set those aside. Take the selenite and circle it around yourself to cleanse your energy. Circle the amethyst around your head to open your third eye for mental clarity. Place chrysoprase over your heart for an emotional cleansing. Replace the chrysoprase with the rhodochrosite to amplify the love you have. Set the crystals around you and place the malachite in front of you.

Either lie back or sit up and meditate over the first lists you made and ask yourself if doubt truly has a place in your relationship. Focus on this, then hold the malachite in your hand and say,

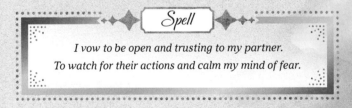

Spell

I vow to be open and trusting to my partner.
To watch for their actions and calm my mind of fear.

Overcome Heartbreak

Heartbreak truly takes after its namesake. It can feel like you're split in two, and the pain can be so debilitating that it's difficult to function. When we're in the throes of pain and suffering, we need to perform shadow work. If none of your usual coping skills or spells are working, then it's time to dig deep, look inside yourself and confront your shadow self. Going into the darkness is the only way through it, and when you're on the other side, healing awaits.

You'll need:

- Frankincense incense for release
- Charged water
- Cauldron
- A tea candle
- Black salt for banishing
- Apache tear for transmuting negative energy into positive energy
- Clear quartz for clarity
- Tiger's eye for self-reliance

Perform this spell during the Waning Moon and as close to midnight as you can. Light the incense and arrange your altar. Pour the charged water into your cauldron. Then place the candle on the water's surface, taking care not to get water onto the candle, and light it. Call on your patron deity and ask them for guidance and protection. Turn off all the lights around you and black out any light coming into the room. You'll want to be in total darkness. Pour your black salt around yourself and the altar to prevent these energies from coming back.

Grab your crystals and sit in front of your altar. Hold on to them and feel their texture. Think of each of their powers and feel the vibrations flow from them to you. Close your eyes and slowly take five deep breaths, inhaling the scent of the incense. With each breath in, imagine a collection of your sadness, and with each breath out, imagine whisking it out of you.

Open your eyes and focus on the light emitting from the cauldron. Just as there's darkness surrounding your world right now, there is also light. Say this,

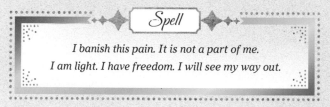

Spell

I banish this pain. It is not a part of me.
I am light. I have freedom. I will see my way out.

Do this as many times as you need to.

Self-empowerment After Pain Spell

When a relationship ends, our egos take a hit. The expected life path is to be partnered up, get married, and have kids. Faced with that, the easiest thing to do is self-criticize. That's not the witch's way! Your self-worth isn't tied to being in a relationship. This spell will take you back to your roots and remind you of who you are.

Gather:

- An outfit that makes you feel confident
- Tissue paper
- Scissors
- An indelible or consecrated pen
- Dragon's blood resin for self-love
- Allspice for courage
- Clove for new beginnings
- Orange peel for truth
- Parsley for strength
- 2 tablespoons of sand
- Cauldron
- Tongs
- A charcoal disc
- A hand mirror
- An orange candle for happiness
- A green candle for luck

Perform this spell any time in between the First Quarter Moon and the Full Moon. Put on the outfit that makes you feel the most confident in yourself. This will be your cloak protecting you and amplifying you. Cut out a piece of tissue paper big enough to hold the herbs and spices. Draw a sigil on the paper and then place the herbs and spices on it. Twist the corners of the paper together so that it seals.

Put the sand in the cauldron. Take the tongs and hold the charcoal disc so that the rounded half is facing out. Do not touch it after being lit; it will burn you. Light the bottom of the disc until it sparks, then place it on the sand. Place the tissue paper bundle atop the disc, then let the energies of the herbs release into the air.

Go back toward your altar with the hand mirror and light the candles. Using their light, look at your reflection. Gaze into it until you see yourself for what you are. Then say,

Spell

I see myself as I am.
Powerful, wonderful, complete.
I am enough on my own.

Fresh Start Elixir Spray

Discontent or arguments can create instability in the home. Emotionally charged moments and things left unsaid leave negative energies hanging in the air, making your sanctuary feel unsafe. In this case, an energy cleansing is vital to return your space to normalcy. With this spray, you'll reform the atmosphere of your home into something peaceful once again.

What you'll need:

◆ A small glass spray bottle
◆ Witch hazel for self-love and as the emulsifier
◆ 3 drops of sage oil for purification
◆ 3 drops of chamomile oil for peace
◆ 1 drop of oregano oil for clearing negative energy
◆ Distilled water

Perform this spell on a Sunday during the Waning Moon. Sunday is the day for success and new beginnings. Take the spray bottle and fill it about halfway with witch hazel. Then pour the correct number of drops for each essential oil. If the smell is too light, feel free to add more until you're satisfied. Pour in the distilled water to top off the elixir. Give it three shakes to mix everything together.

Next, open all the windows in your domicile. If it's a windy day, even better! Place yourself in the middle of your home and breathe in and out with the air current. As you breathe in, imagine collecting the dark energies and breathing them back out. Picture your house as if it's breathing with you. When you feel the negative energies are gone, take the elixir and begin spraying it all around. Get every space, especially the places where you have the most negative associations. As you spray, say,

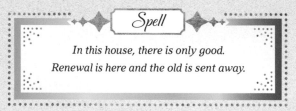

Spell

In this house, there is only good.
Renewal is here and the old is sent away.

Repeat this spell until Tuesday, the day of success and personal power.

4
Family, Friends, and Animals

P LATONIC LOVE IS ONE OF THE MOST fulfilling and plentiful types of love. Our first experiences with love are platonic, rather than romantic, and continue throughout our lives in the form of our parents, siblings, and extended family. It stretches to our community and our animal companions. This type of love doesn't get as much attention, but it's just as important as romantic love. Both require quality time, understanding, joy, and thoughtfulness to flourish.

With friends and family, and even pets, we are encouraged to be as open with our love as possible, and take creative measures to show it. Within this section, you'll learn to bring your platonic loves in for a celebration in your garden. Just as Mother Nature is diverse, so are we and the friendships we share. For example, some of the herbs discussed in this chapter are apple, sweet pea, and myrtle; most people don't think of friendship when they hear those names, but that's what makes them so delightful.

In the following pages, you'll learn to create dragon's blood ink to use to write letters to friends to show that you care. You'll delight in Nature with your family as a way to get closer to them. You'll craft a potpourri bag for the health and happiness of your friends. It's a remarkably discreet way of blessing someone with magic. Last, you'll experiment with animal magic as a way to welcome a new pet, be more connected with the animal kingdom, and bond with your familiar.

Lemon Balm Love Spell

When family harmony is needed and friends and family need tending, choose lemon balm to ward away evil, ushering in health and love. Smelling sweetly of grass and lemon, this steady herb thrives most anywhere it's planted, setting roots that spread and establishing friends and family easily, of which lemon balm speaks fondly. Its stubborn optimism is hard to ignore; it's comforting words a friend.

Lemon balm's scent is instantly uplifting and cheerful. Use an infusion to clean any room in the home that needs to be cleared of negative energy, such as after an illness, argument, or other negative experience. A joyful spirit will return. Sprinkle on a salad to entice a lover.

To soothe a troubled spirit, hang a few sprigs, especially those just about to flower, on a mirror. Gaze into the mirror, honoring your innate goddess, and say quietly or aloud:

Spell

O' sacred herb, release in me your sweet uplifting joy,
to ease my fears and calm my tears and wash them from my eyes.

Dragon's Blood Letter

There's something inherently magical about words. They have the power to tear down but, more importantly, to uplift and enrich any friendship. What better way to express friendship than in a letter? We live in a time where you can send a message at any time to your friends, but there's nothing like a good handwritten letter to tell your friends how much you appreciate them. And dragon's blood is the perfect ink for the job. It is associated with love and will enhance any written spell or pact. You can buy a bottle of it online or make some yourself.

When crafting your letter, use this formula:

♦ Greet your friend and tell them you've been thinking about them.
♦ Tell them why you're writing this letter.
♦ Tell them how much you appreciate them, then tell them what goals you want for your friendship.

That last part is your intention, and the part of the spell that's the most powerful. When sealing the letter, feel free to use a red or pink wax seal to represent how much you care for your friendship.

Enchanted Basil Balsamic Vinegar

Spice up your mealtime routine with a dash of basil balsamic. This sweet, earthy vinegar is beautifully complemented by this aromatic herb. Basil's magical properties are good for, among other things, fostering family love and boosting luck. For more than just salads, dress grilled meats or vegetables, drizzle over fresh tomatoes and mozzarella or pizza, or dip in a crusty bread or fresh vegetables for a flavor-filled appetizer and a peaceful family meal.

You will need:

- ♦ Two 28-ounce (720-ml) Mason jars with their lids
- ♦ 1 cup (35 g) packed basil leaves, gently washed and thoroughly dried (water promotes bacterial growth)
- ♦ 2 cups (480 ml) balsamic vinegar, plus more as needed (use a good-quality vinegar for best results)
- ♦ Fine-mesh sieve and bowl to strain

1. Wash and thoroughly dry the Mason jars and their lids.
2. Gently bruise or crush the basil to help release the oils.
3. Place the basil in one jar, leaving 1 to 2 inches (2.5 to 5 cm) of space at the top.

4. Pour the vinegar over the basil, almost filling the jar.

5. Cover the jar with its lid and set aside in a cool, dark place for up to two weeks.

6. After three or four days, taste the vinegar to judge how intense the herbal flavor is. You may want to taste it each day until it develops to your desired depth of basil flavor.

7. Place a fine-mesh sieve over a clean, dry bowl and strain the vinegar into it.

8. Transfer the basil balsamic to the second 28-ounce (720-ml) jar and seal the lid tightly.

9. Store in a cool, dark place for up to one year. If the vinegar shows any signs of change or deterioration, such as mold growth, discard immediately and do not use. If mealtime madness has you in its spell, recast the energy to bring everyone to the table at once by reciting these words:

Spell

Sweet basil spin your magic charms, a call to gather 'round
To share the meal presented here, when family time abounds.
No chat, or text, or Instamess . . . it's you I long to see.
So, grab a chair, a fork, a pear!, and tell me how you've been.

Family Blessings of the Goddess Spell

Appeal to your favorite matriarch goddess for her guidance and blessings to keep watch over your family. When ready, say quietly or aloud:

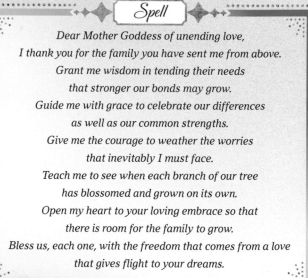

Spell

Dear Mother Goddess of unending love,
I thank you for the family you have sent me from above.
Grant me wisdom in tending their needs
that stronger our bonds may grow.
Guide me with grace to celebrate our differences
as well as our common strengths.
Give me the courage to weather the worries
that inevitably I must face.
Teach me to see when each branch of our tree
has blossomed and grown on its own.
Open my heart to your loving embrace so that
there is room for the family to grow.
Bless us, each one, with the freedom that comes from a love
that gives flight to your dreams.

Family Blessings of the Moon Spell

In this natural period of rest and renewal, now is the time to reconnect with friends and family you may have neglected during busier times. This simple spell can help you send loving vibrations out into the Universe. Say it quietly or aloud as many times as you like, and keep watch for what returns to you.

Spell

In times of darkness, friendships shine bright.
In times of darkness, family holds tight.
In times like these, when Moon's light wanes,
tend carefully to love that sustains.
O' Goddess Moon, O' mother of night,
shine tenderly your protecting light.

Make an Offering to Corn Mother

Call on Corn Mother, the Goddess of Marriage, Fertility, and Motherhood, to nourish you in any way that sustains. Corn Mother's selfless love is one of nourishment and acceptance. She is the mother we all know who feeds us constantly as a sign of her care and adoration. She readily shares all she has, including her wisdom, that we may lead productive lives.

Offerings

Corn—in all its forms. Keep a dried ear of corn on your altar to channel Corn Mother's protective energies. Cornstalk dolls are a favorite. Fill your cauldron with clean soil and sprinkle some seeds on top as a gift to Corn Mother. Clean water and sunlight are also welcome, as they nurture the corn toward full growth.

Spell

O Mother Goddess who gives life,
in thankfulness I bow tonight.
With outstretched arms to honor you,
to sing the praise of all you do.
I ask your blessing of my life,
to love and marry—and breathe life
into the plans we've made today
to conquer fear and challenge strife.
To see the cycle start anew,
each precious gift is born of you.
The fruits of labor reaped this way engage
my soul and light the way.

Make an Offering to Frigg

Seek the wisdom of Frigg, the Goddess of Home, Hearth, and Healing, in matters of hearth and home. Invite her in any time your goddess energies are running low. Call on Frigg to restore a balance of power when things seem to be out of sync, or skills of diplomacy are needed to reach agreement. Devotees also sought help regarding domestic crafts and cottage industries. If you have a home-based business or are sole proprietor of a business, put Frigg on your board.

Frigg's powers were most closely aligned with matters of marriage and all things home and family. She is also an independent woman, able to be partner, mother, friend, and wife while keeping her own identity fully intact. She is extremely clever and uses this power to her advantage. She also had the power to foretell the future, blessed with the wisdom to keep her secrets—though she was believed to be weaver of the fates as a result.

Offerings

Keep your altar to Frigg clean and tidy and place upon it offerings of wine or wool. Spend some time volunteering to help other women; make peace in your family where it's needed; retake your marriage vows. Clean your house!

Spell

*Goddess, please do share your spell
to dampen swift each fire that swells.
So, buoyed I be by your great charms
that never will my home know harm,
Just joy and bounty far and wide—
each reaped with gratitude and pride.
This home and hearth, dear goddess, bless,
that love and time reveal our best.*

Entryway Blessing

It is believed by the Irish that upon entering a new home, you must also leave through the same door to ensure luck flows into the home . . . except at the witching hour on New Year's Eve, when in the front and out the back you must go to sweep in a lucky new year.

Set the tone for your home and life with a welcome mat or sign so that all feel love who enter.

Spell

This home abounds with life and love and welcomes all who come.
For multiplied these joys do thrive when shared by more than one.
The love and laughter echo on and, yes, the house does smile.

Welcoming New Friends

New friendships expand our souls and our homes. When new friendships blossom, a simple welcoming spell can set the energies in motion. Sit quietly in the room where friends and family gather most, such as a den, living room, or playroom. Wear or hold clear quartz or rose quartz to enhance the friendly vibrations, or garnet to help send your inviting message into the world to be received by others. Recite:

Spell

Friends. Gather. Home. Filled.
Hearts. Matter. Cares. Stilled.
Love. Nurture. Lives. Build.

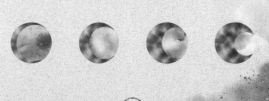

Season Your Life
with Friendship

Gather your friends on a Sun-filled day to celebrate the
bounty of your garden—or just to celebrate the bounty of your
friendship. Have plenty of herbs—fresh, dried, potted or plotted—
on hand that support love and friendship, encourage growth
and open communication, and that are just joyous to experience
and behold. Kitchen gifts of food and wine made with fresh
herbs will enhance the celebratory spirit of the circle. Consider
including these herbs in your herbal friendship ritual, whose
energies attract and maintain friendship, or speak the language
of friendship:

♦ Apples   ♦ Lemons   ♦ Rosemary

♦ Cloves   ♦ Myrtle   ♦ Sweet pea

♦ Lavender   ♦ Oak-leaved geranium   ♦ Zinnia, for

♦ Lemon balm   ♦ Rose   absent friends

Cast a ritual circle by strewing herbs and blossoms around your
gathering area. Casting is simply connecting with the energies of
the Earth and the Universe. Invite your friends to step inside the
circle to connect and amplify their energies by joining hands.

If you like, each person can place an herbal offering inside the circle. The purpose of your circle is to celebrate and honor the goddess, Mother Earth, and all her gifts and to open yourself to her energies, increasing vibration and intuition. Invite her to join you in the circle.

Use the circle for intention-setting. Create and chant your own mantra to raise the energies around you. Stand or sit silently in meditation on your intentions. Sing, walk, or dance clockwise in the circle. Why clockwise? The spinning clockwise energy brings things to you. Share intentions aloud, or offer them quietly to the Universe. When it is time to close the circle, light a candle in memory of someone unable to be there and take a moment to give thanks for the seasonal blessings of the Earth and your friends. Walk or dance counterclockwise to dissolve the circle.

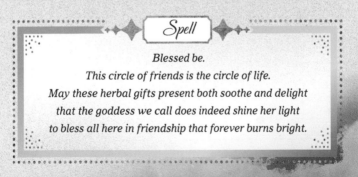

Spell

Blessed be.
This circle of friends is the circle of life.
May these herbal gifts present both soothe and delight
that the goddess we call does indeed shine her light
to bless all here in friendship that forever burns bright.

Celebrating Differences

The thrilling diversity of the herbal kingdom is something
we celebrate and yearn to learn more about, and so it should
be with the uplifting diversity of the human kingdom. When
differences threaten to divide instead of delight, learning more
about them is the first step to understanding differences aren't
always as different as they first appear. Gather cinquefoil,
mugwort, sage, and willow for wisdom; morning glory and
rosemary for acceptance; sweet pea for friendship; and
nasturtium for working in harmony. Invite the wisdom of your
favorite goddess in for a chat. When ready to seek common
ground, say quietly or aloud:

Spell

*These herbs in friendship offered are, with purest of intent
to let the conversation flow, to understand what's meant
by words and deeds, to sow the seeds of wisdom
and accept what's different.*

Clove Herbal Friendship Spell

Clove speaks of dignity, and it benefits a friendship by providing an open and safe atmosphere, free of judgement. It is frequently used to invite prosperity, protection, and purification energies. Clove's scent can open your intuition and create a sense of openness in meditation.

Use clove essential oil to improve memory, friendship, and safety. A necklace of cloves can be worn as a protective measure. When clove is burned, it will stop people from gossiping about you, will draw money to you, and banish negative energy from you. Tuck into poppets, spell jars, and posies for any of its applicable properties, depending on your needs. Given to friends, clove will keep the friendship strong.

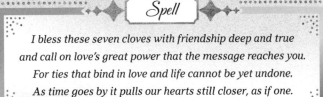

Spell

*I bless these seven cloves with friendship deep and true
and call on love's great power that the message reaches you.
For ties that bind in love and life cannot be yet undone.
As time goes by it pulls our hearts still closer, as if one.*

Friendship Moon Spell

If it's companionship you yearn for, the Waxing Moon can be your spell's best friend.

Gather a red or pink candle and matches. Sit comfortably in a quiet place and light the candle on a heatproof surface. Gaze at the flame. Let your mind be free while the light fills you with peace. Taking long slow breaths—in and out—visualize activities you might do with your new friend, someone like-minded who enjoys doing the same things as you. When you feel ready, say quietly or aloud:

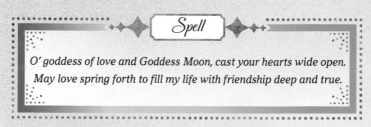

Spell

O' goddess of love and Goddess Moon, cast your hearts wide open. May love spring forth to fill my life with friendship deep and true.

Repeat as many times as you like. Let the candle burn down as you continue to visualize you and your new friend together. Keep your energies open to meeting new people.

Giving Thanks

The Full Moon fills us to the brim. Take a moment to give thanks and a nod of gratitude for the bounty in your life—then pass it on. Say quietly or aloud:

Spell

I thank you, Moon, for all you do to guide and comfort me.
I thank you, friends, for all you give—your love, support, and glee.
And so I stand beneath your light with heart so full of love,
To know my life is blessed, you see, without you I have none.

Rosemary-infused Olive Oil Ritual

Rosemary typically symbolizes remembrance, but it can also attract romantic love and protection. So, what better potion for creating delicious memories than a dose of rosemary oil? Add to your favorite foods, or pass a little magic to your friends when you give this as a gift. Whatever you choose, it will be unforgettable.

♦ 2 pint-size (480 ml) Mason jars with lids
♦ 6 rosemary sprigs, gently washed, dried, and left out overnight to thoroughly dry (water promotes bacterial growth), damaged leaves removed
♦ 1 cup (240 ml) olive oil, plus more as needed
♦ Fine-mesh sieve and bowl to strain

1. Wash and thoroughly dry the Mason jars and their lids.

2. Gently bruise or crush the rosemary sprigs to help release their oils.

3. Place the rosemary in one jar, leaving 1 to 2 inches (2.5 to 5 cm) of space at the top.

4. Pour the olive oil over the rosemary, covering the herbs by at least 1 inch (2.5 cm).

5. Cover the jar with a lid and set aside in a cool, dark place for up to one week.

6. After three or four days, taste the oil to judge how intense the herbal flavor is. You may want to taste it each day until it develops your desired depth of rosemary flavor.

7. Place a fine-mesh sieve over a clean, dry bowl and strain the oil into it.

8. Transfer the rosemary oil to the second pint-size (480 ml) jar and seal the lid tightly.

9. Keep refrigerated for up to one month. If the oil shows any signs of change or deterioration, such as mold growth, discard immediately and do not use. Bring to room temperature to use.

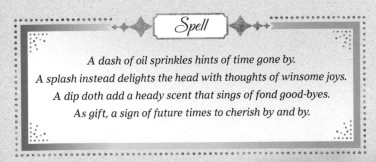

Spell

A dash of oil sprinkles hints of time gone by.
A splash instead delights the head with thoughts of winsome joys.
A dip doth add a heady scent that sings of fond good-byes.
As gift, a sign of future times to cherish by and by.

Orange Blossom Friendship Spell

Orange blossom attracts friendship, love, luck, joy, and abundance and stirs up a sunny outlook on life. Like the deliciously refreshing fruit the flower becomes, orange blossom uplifts, soothes, and rejuvenates.

Carry orange blossom in a wedding bouquet to ensure wedded bliss. Add to potpourri to be given as gifts of friendship to cement the bond. Use orange flower water as part of your facial cleansing routine for a fresh start to each day. Dress an orange candle with orange essential oil before burning to ease the blues and let the sunshine in. Wear orange blossom to attract luck and love to you.

Spell

A whiff of orange from blossom true
does signal sweet my love for you.
These petals tossed upon us rain
like tears of joy, a sweet refrain,
our marriage sealed, it's ever true,
this rare unending love of two.

Animal Companion Blessing

New animal-friend in your home? Here's some help to inspire the perfect name for your new family member. Hold the wiggly bundle in your arms and feel the warmth and energy meld with yours. Let it fill you with wonder that such a small creature can offer such immense love and trust.

Spell

Your eyes so bright, with love and hope they shine.
Your ears and tail do shiver and shake—not to mention your behind!
A name you need by which to heed the call from all your fans—
a name befitting royalty, for soon you'll be the star.
Of neighborhood and play dates, too, and backyard jamborees ...
I have the perfect name in mind, which I bestow on you.

Animal Kingdom

Many goddesses have faithful animal companions ever by their side—to love them, protect them, adorn them, transport them, amuse them, and more! To ensure your beloved animal companions stay healthy, safe, and happy, evoke any goddess who shares your animal passion. When ready, say quietly or aloud:

Spell

A prayer for all the animals,
upon the Earth who roam,
their gentle love, a gift so pure,
there's none that can compare.
Please bless my sweet companions
for their ever-faithful ways—
an endless well of love that pours each
day from doting eyes.

Welcoming a New Pet

A new pet definitely means a new beginning . . . new habits, new fun, new discoveries, new love, just to name a few. Use the light and energy of the New Moon to recognize and welcome this new family member.

Gather your squirming bundle in your arms and stand somewhere, inside or out, where the Moon's light will reach you. With admiration for the journey you are about to engage in, say quietly or aloud:

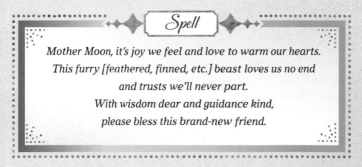

Spell

Mother Moon, it's joy we feel and love to warm our hearts.
This furry [feathered, finned, etc.] beast loves us no end
and trusts we'll never part.
With wisdom dear and guidance kind,
please bless this brand-new friend.

Familiar Bonding

Animals are a miracle of this Earth. They live by the rules of Nature and some of them allow us into their worlds and lives for good. Every witch needs a companion, and animals make the best familiars. They enrich our lives and remind us that we're not the only ones who inhabit the land.

Just as we need to bond with the people in our lives, we also need to connect with our beloved animals. Whether they're a new pet, or an animal you see frequently, you can silently communicate with them and strengthen your relationship. This spell will work best with an animal who is already familiar with you.

To begin, go where you usually see your companion. Carry clear quartz and aquamarine crystals in your pocket for clearing the mind and promoting healthy relationships. Animals are susceptible to mood changes, so you'll want to be as calm as possible. Let your familiar come to you.

When your friend has made their way over to you, look them in the eye, meeting them where they're at. As you lock eyes, focus on how much you love and appreciate them in your life. If they come closer to you, reach out your hand where it's still in their line of sight. Let them sniff you, and if you can, pet them. As you do, let the feelings you have for them flow into your hand. Imagine your aura combining with theirs. Say quietly or aloud,

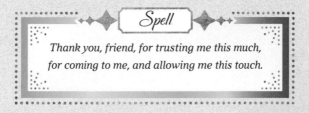

Spell

Thank you, friend, for trusting me this much,
for coming to me, and allowing me this touch.

You'll feel the mood shift. When it does, feel gratitude for Nature and this amazing communion.

Health and Happiness Potpourri Bundle

Love, in all its forms, is about wanting the best for others. When someone is healthy and happy, they can accomplish anything. Contentment is possible, a more gracious life is attainable, and an open heart will leave room for more relationships.

The people in our lives may not understand our witchery or its effects, but there's a way to bless them so they can still receive the benefits. A potpourri bundle of fresh herbs will give off the scent of your intention and provide your friend with an uplifting gift made from the heart. This bundle works similar to a charm bag, but is more discreet and on a larger scale.

What you'll need:

♦ A dash of dill for manifestation
♦ Lemon balm for emotional wellness
♦ Cornflower for happiness
♦ Sage for health
♦ Lavender for peace
♦ Saffron for love
♦ A medium or large tulle drawstring bag (or potpourri vase)

For this spell, take each herb out of its container and feel them with your whole hands. Let them fall between your fingers, hold them in your palms, and even breathe them in. Whatever your association with each herb, let them wash over you. Place each herb strategically in the bag so that they're aesthetically pleasing to you and your friend. You can also buy a potpourri vase to make the gift that much more special. When you give the gift, do it in person to allow a clean transfer directly from you to them.

Communing with Family in Mother Nature

Something about being in Mother Nature tends to grab our attention. She is the mother from whom we came, the one who exists, whether we remember her or not. Because she is our genesis, it's crucial to return to her every now again for renewal and communion. Who better to share this with than family? Being around family reminds us of our roots, gives us a sense of community, and a place to call home. Mother Nature aims to share herself with you and your loved ones, chosen or otherwise.

Preparation for this spell must happen days in advance. It might be tricky, but you'll need to coordinate with everyone for a common time and location. Ideally, this will be a place that has meaning for everyone, but the spell can still work in an unfamiliar yet stunning place. Next, pay close attention to the weather in your area and choose a clear, sunny day.

The night before, make a small charm bag to keep on your person.

You'll need:

- A yellow pouch or drawstring bag
- Gold for happiness
- Mugwort for communication with Spirit
- Basil for squabble-free love
- Lavender for awareness

Take the pouch and place it on your windowsill so that when you wake up, it's been charged by sunrise. The sunrise symbolizes new beginnings and refreshment. Before you head out, say this prayer to the Sun:

Spell

Father Sun, thank you for opening the sky just for me.
Show my family your splendor and that of Mother Nature.

Go with your family to your chosen destination and focus on being together. Whether playing games, talking, or quietly relaxing, choose to be in the moment with them and let the elements do the rest.

Friendship Talisman

The ancient Greeks had many words for love, including *philia*, which means "friendship love," or brotherly love. One aspect of philia is the desire to protect your friends. As they go about life, there are so many sources of evil and harm that can affect them without their knowledge. Invisible influences exist everywhere, and your friends won't always have you to look out for them. Unfortunately, you can't be with them all the time. What you can do is give them a talisman. A talisman is an object intended to protect and heal the wearer, which is precisely what yours will do.

You will need these materials:

- A small piece of paper
- An indelible or consecrated pen
- A small glass vial with a cork
- Frankincense incense for purification
- Dried daisy for friendship
- Cinnamon for protection
- Hematite chip for absorbing negative energies and transforming them into strength
- Yellow quartz for happiness
- A small hook eye
- Hot glue gun and glue
- A black chain or leather strap for the necklace

First, on the small piece of paper draw the Hagalaz rune. It's meant to banish negative influences and help us through difficult times. Place your thumb on the rune and close your eyes. Focus your energy on the rune, feeling its lines on your skin. Your intention will combine with the rune's innate power, and it will make it stronger.

Next, cleanse the vial with incense. Then, drop the herbs into the vial one at a time, filling it about a fourth of the way. Place the rune inside, followed by the crystals. Take the hook eye and stick it into the cork, adding some glue to it. Take the hot glue gun and carefully trace the lip of the vial. Place the cork.

Now, thread your strap of choice through the hook. When gifting the talisman to your friend, deliver it to them in a white bag or box for the purity of your intentions.

Conclusion

Now that you've completed this book, you have the tools to share the greatest gift you can give another person. After flowing through the pages, you've learned how to find love, keep your partnerships going strong, navigate through trauma, and celebrate the platonic love in your life. You've come to the end much wiser than before. With this new knowledge, you can adjust, add, or blend any or all of the spells you see in this book. Just like love, magic is tailored to each person and their specific circumstances. We hope you take what you've learned and add your unique spin to the spells and rituals listed! Magic is suggestive and what matters the most are your associations with the goddesses, herbs, flowers, and crystals mentioned in this book. The possibilities are endless.

Though this is a book on love, it's important to keep in mind that love, as a whole, is not a strain. Practicing witchcraft isn't all that's required to find or have love. It's something that comes to you when you're ready. Spells and charms increase your chances at finding and keeping love, but don't forget that witchcraft is also supplemental. It requires us to perform in the right mindset; it's also up to Spirit and the Universe. Don't rush love, and don't be discouraged if the spells don't work exactly as you envisioned or as quickly as you wanted. Good things take time. Take comfort in the fact that the witches who crafted this book went through the ups and downs of love ourselves. We've consulted the goddesses, gotten our hearts broken, lived, learned, and now we've come far enough to give you hope and advice. Take as much or as little of it as you need. No matter what you choose, may you find love, always.

So Mote It Be.

Spell Index

Brimming with creative inspiration, how-to projects, and useful information to enrich your everyday life, quarto.com is a favorite destination for those pursuing their interests and passions.

Library of Congress Cataloging-in-Publication Data

Names: Radcliffe, Minerva, author.
Title: Love spells : an enchanting spell book of potions & rituals / by Minerva Radcliffe.
Description: New York, NY : Wellfleet Press, 2022. | Series: Pocket spell
  books | Summary: "Love Spells is a pocket-size volume of potions,
  charms, and spells that can help you find love, maintain relationships,
  or reconnect with old friends"-- Provided by publisher.
Identifiers: LCCN 2021057030 (print) | LCCN 2021057031 (ebook) | ISBN
  9781577153146 (hardcover) | ISBN 9780760376386 (ebook)
Subjects: LCSH: Magic. | Love--Miscellanea. | Charms. | Incantations.
Classification: LCC BF1623.L6 L68 2022 (print) | LCC BF1623.L6 (ebook) |
  DDC 133.4/42--dc23/eng/20220107
LC record available at https://lccn.loc.gov/2021057030
LC ebook record available at https://lccn.loc.gov/2021057031

Publisher: Rage Kindelsperger
Creative Director: Laura Drew
Managing Editor: Cara Donaldson
Project Editor: Sara Bonacum
Cover and Interior Design: Evelin Kasikov

Printed in China